Critters Don't Litter
~ A Littering Story ~

Adele A. Roberts

www.CrittersDontLitter.com

CONTENTS

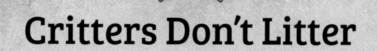

Critters Don't Litter

Have you ever seen a critter litter?

What a strange sight that would be.

Critters, big and small, throwing things for all to see.

If I saw a critter litter, I'd tell him it's not right.

"Critter, don't throw litter, it makes a terrible sight.

Who is going to clean it up? It really isn't fair.

Will you pick it up or don't you care?"

BUT, Critters don't litter! They are clean as they can be.

Throwing things around is not for them, you see.

It's people who throw litter and don't seem to care,

They fill our country full of litter and just leave it there.

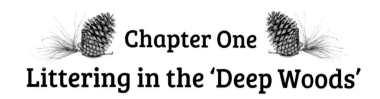

Chapter One
Littering in the 'Deep Woods'

Sammy the skunk visited the 'deep woods' often. He did not live there, but it was a very special place where he had many animal friends. Sammy was a very well-educated skunk and helped the animals solve problems that arose in the deep woods. He became a hero to them.

There was one path that only animals were allowed to take into the deep woods. It was guarded by Mr. and Mrs. Owl who watched and warned the animals of approaching dangers. Humans never entered the woods because it was overgrown with trees, bushes and vines.

Whenever Sammy was needed, his friend Mr. Fox, would stand at the edge of the deep woods and wave his tail. This was a signal for Sammy to come.

The animals loved the deep woods. They felt safe and everything they needed was there. Every animal family was proud to take care of their home. When spring came the animals would get together and have a 'clean up'. All the dead leaves were trampled on so they would make a soft carpet to walk on, and the dead branches were gathered to make homes.

One morning as Mr. and Mrs. Owl were flying around the open land they became alarmed when they saw humans. Tents had been set up and a fire had been built. Mr. and Mrs. Owl watched them for a while before heading back to the woods. As they were the caretakers of the woods they immediately told Mr. Fox what they had seen. The main concern was that the humans would find a way into the deep woods.

Mr. Fox listened carefully to Mr. and Mrs. Owl as they told him about the humans. "I believe we must be careful. We will tell all our animal friends to be quiet and on the alert. We can watch the humans from a distance. I'm going to let Sammy know about this," said Mr. Fox.

Mr. Fox went to the edge of the woods and waved his tail for Sammy to see. Soon Sammy and Mr. Fox were walking in the deep woods and Mr. Fox explained to Sammy about the humans. The owls had already alerted the other animals and now they were waiting for Sammy. They knew Sammy would know what to do.

After hearing about the humans being so close, Sammy agreed with the advice Mr. Fox had given. "We will watch them from a distance," assured Sammy.

The animals gathered at the edge of the woods. They saw something they didn't understand. The humans picked up something, threw something on the ground, and then put something in their mouths. They opened something, drank from it and threw it on the ground. They lit something, put it in their mouths where smoke came out of it, and then threw it on the ground. They opened up bags of things and threw them on the ground. It wasn't long before the ground around them was covered with things. Mrs. Owl asked Mr. Owl, "What are they doing?"

Before he could answer, Sammy spoke, "Mrs. Owl, humans eat differently than we do. Everything is wrapped or bottled or bagged. When they are young they are taught to throw things into trash cans or plastic garbage bags and then later take it to a place where all of it is buried or sometimes burned. This keeps everything tidy in their world."

"But where are the trash cans and plastic bags? I don't see any," exclaimed Mrs. Owl.

"They may have them somewhere. I'm sure they wouldn't just leave everything on the ground," remarked Sammy.

All the animals strained their eyes to see what the humans were going to do with all the 'things' they had thrown on the ground.

Time went by and soon the humans packed up their tents, put out the fire, and left. Not one thing was picked up.

Mrs. Owl looked sad when she asked Sammy, "They didn't learn to use trash cans or plastic garbage bags did they?"

"I'm afraid no one ever taught them what the right thing is to do," replied Sammy.

The animals saw what the humans left on the ground and hung their heads. With tears in her eyes, Mrs. Owl said, "Our land isn't beautiful anymore is it?"

They watched for some time, thinking that the humans would come back and pick up the 'things' that were on the ground.

Finally Mr. Owl spoke up, "I believe we should all go back to our homes now. There is really nothing we can do."

The animals quietly and slowly walked away. Mr. Fox went with Sammy to the edge of the deep woods where they said their good-byes.

Chapter Two
ANDY COMES TO VISIT

When Sammy got home his mother and father were waiting for him and could hardly wait to tell him the news. "We have a surprise for you Sammy! Your cousin, Andy, is coming today! We expect him any time now. Why don't you go outside and watch for him."

Sammy hadn't seen his cousin for some time and wondered why he was visiting. He knew that Andy was a little older than he and was also very well-educated.

It wasn't too long before Sammy saw Andy coming toward the house.

"Hi, Sammy! It's me – Andy! How are you doing? Say, it's good to see you!"

"I'm fine Andy. You look great. It's good to see you too," said Sammy.

"Tell me what you have been up to Sammy. Is there anything that I should know about?" remarked Andy.

Sammy was anxious to tell Andy about the deep woods and all his friends that live there, but before he could say anything, Andy spoke!

"Sammy, I've been appointed to a very important position by the Animal Environmental Protection Agency! I have been taught many things about littering, and I am to teach others what I have learned. Do you know what 'littering' means?" asked Andy.

Sammy was amazed. "I can't believe this Andy! Yes, I do know about littering because I learned about it in school. Just today we saw littering by humans near the 'deep woods'.

Looking very puzzled, Andy asked, "The deep woods? What is that, Sammy?"

Sammy pointed to a very dark wooded area that looked like no one could enter because of all the overgrown trees, bushes, and vines.

"You mean, you go into a place like that? How can you? I'd stay far away from it!" remarked Andy.

Sammy laughed. "Andy, it is a very special place. There is a path that you can take to get into the woods. Mr. and Mrs. Owl live in a tree and guard the path. I'm going to take you there."

"If I go with you, I wouldn't be in any danger would I?" asked Andy.

"Oh no!" said Sammy. "You will be welcomed by all my animal friends. Come on – let's go and I'll show you what we saw today."

Soon they stood under the home of Mr. and Mrs. Owl. Mr. Owl was sitting outside. He opened his eyes wide and glared down. "Sammy, who is that?" he asked.

Mr. Owl scared Andy and he jumped behind Sammy. "You don't have to be afraid, Andy. Mr. Owl won't hurt you!" said Sammy. "Mr. Owl, I am very proud to introduce my cousin, Andy. He comes from the city and is here for a visit. He works for the Animal Environmental Protection Agency."

Mrs. Owl heard what was being said and came out of their home to see who Mr. Owl was talking to. "Oh my, that is just wonderful! What do you do? You know we are sort of a protection agency also! We protect all the animals in the deep woods."

Andy was no longer frightened. He began to tell about his work to Mr. and Mrs. Owl. Sammy listened carefully.

"I have been taught several things about littering. My job is to teach what happens when people litter. Sammy told me that you saw humans throwing things on your beautiful land and leaving it on the ground. Will you show me where they littered by your deep woods?" asked Andy.

Mr. Fox saw Mr. and Mrs. Owl flying above him and then noticed Sammy and a strange skunk walking together. He quickly went to see where they were going. Sammy was happy to see his friend Mr. Fox. He introduced him to his cousin Andy, and then asked Mr. Fox if he would like to join them.

"We're going to show Andy where the humans put all those things," said Sammy. "He knows a great deal about littering and he is going to teach us all about it."

Mrs. Owl spoke up, "Mr. Owl and I are very wise and we also know that littering looks awful, but we don't know much about it."

"Don't you worry about that Mrs. Owl, you'll soon know a great deal," explained Andy.

The animals continued walking and soon came to a clearing where the humans had been.

Andy was not surprised at the amount of litter that was spread on the ground. He had seen it many times before and each time he wondered 'why'?

After looking at a countryside that now looked like a dump, Andy asked to go back to the deep woods to see if he could talk to all the animals.

Mr. and Mrs. Owl flew throughout the woods and told the animals to gather at the lake.

Chapter Three
ANDY TEACHES ABOUT LITTERING

Andy stood before a very large group of animals. There were raccoons, beavers, deer, squirrels, rabbits, opossums, groundhogs and even turtles! He felt a little intimidated when the bear families came waddling in to hear what he was going to say. However, he knew he had a job to do and so he began.

"First I want you to know that critters don't litter!" He looked into the eyes of the animals staring at him. "However, people DO! You saw what they did today. Can I change what they did? NO. Why you may ask do they litter? Well, let me try to explain."

"Most people do not litter. It is disgusting to them to see litter along the roadsides and in other places. They dislike it when litter is thrown into their yards and neighborhoods. It looks awful and it stinks! However, there are careless people who do litter. These people may simply not care and it doesn't matter to them. It could be they feel it isn't their responsibility. They may have never been taught that littering is wrong. They

never realized it could harm animals, people, or the environment. You may be wondering what harm littering does. It could be very dangerous. If you come upon litter you must remember to be very careful and don't go near it. Even if you think there is something you'd like to eat – DON'T. Animals have gotten their heads caught in cans and plastic bags and have smothered. The litter could also be rotten and you could get sick or die. Then there is always the possibility that you could cut yourself on broken glass or other things that are sharp."

Andy continued, "Is there any animal here that knows anything about money?"

Sammy spoke up, "I know that people work, get money so they can buy the things they need. Money comes in coins and paper bills!"

"You're right, Sammy!" commended Andy.

"Let me tell you how expensive 'littering' is," explained Andy.

Mrs. Owl was very interested and asked, "Do humans have to buy litter with money?"

Andy smiled as he answered, "No, but let me tell you how much money humans spend each year to take care of the litter that is thrown on highways, country sides, parks, school grounds and other places where littering is seen. It costs people who live in the United States approximately 11.5 billion dollars each year to clean it up! Who cleans it up? People are hired or clean litter up themselves. About 50 billion pieces of litter are picked up each year. AND as many as 6,500 items are picked up every mile!"

"Oh my!" that is disgraceful said Mrs. Owl. "What can be done?"

"People have to change their attitude about littering," said Andy. "I am teaching you now, and I'd like you to remember what I am telling you, but how people feel about throwing things on the ground and leaving them is important. Many people do not know what they are doing when they litter. They do not realize that it is entirely up to them to keep the country clean and beautiful."

"Who does most of the littering?" asked Mr. Fox.
"Most littering is done by children, teen-agers and young adults who are in their twenties or thirties. However, some

older adults litter also," answered Andy.

Mr. Bear spoke up, "Are people punished for littering?"

"Absolutely! There are many laws and people who are caught pay fines. These fines could be fifty dollars or as much as twenty-five hundred dollars!" answered Andy.

"What will happen to all of the litter that the humans left behind near our woods?" asked Sammy.

"I would hope a human sees it and picks it up. But, there are other things that could happen to it. If there is a strong wind it could blow away, but it doesn't disappear. It could blow into lawns or landscaped areas, or into storm drains that would lead to waterways like streams, creeks, lakes and oceans. It could kill the fish and other aquatic animals that live there. It could rot and the smell would be horrible," remarked Andy.

One of the little rabbits hopped up to Andy. He put his nose in Andy's face, and asked, "Would the smell be worse than yours?"

All the animals broke out in laughter! Even Sammy and Andy knew this was a good question.

Andy answered without hesitating, "YES! LITTERING STINKS! I mean it REALLY STINKS!"

Andy felt he had told the deep woods animals enough. He asked if there were any more questions before he headed back with Sammy to his home. Andy was going to report back to the Animal Environmental Protection Agency and tell what he saw and what he taught the animals about littering. He waited for questions..

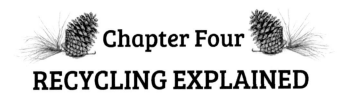

Chapter Four
RECYCLING EXPLAINED

A quiet voice was heard. "Andy, could you tell us what litter is and how it should be taken care of?"

Andy thought for a moment before answering, "Litter is anything that is scattered around carelessly. It is hard to name all the things that people throw on the ground. It could be gum or candy wrappers, bottles, paper items of all kinds, pop cans, cigarettes, food, metal objects, glass and plastic containers or garbage. This is only naming a few items. These should NEVER be thrown on the ground. If a person is wise he/she will have plastic garbage bags in vehicles to place throw-away items, and when they are outside of their home they should look for trash cans to dispose of their litter. In many states there are county convenience centers where people can take their trash without charge. There are also garbage companies who pick it up.

One of the most amazing things people can do is called 'recycling'. People have the opportunity to take some of the litter that they would normally throw away and use it again!" Mr. Turtle nudged his way closer to Andy. The other animals were very considerate and gave him room as he approached Andy. "I have a question, Mr. Andy. If you're talking about stinky litter, why would people want to use it again?"

The other animals were in agreement with the question and thought using litter was a silly thing to do.

Andy knew he had to explain 'recycling' very well so the animals would understand. "Of course, not all litter can be recycled. Yes, there are things that definitely need to be thrown away, but some things can be recycled and used again. I'll give you a list of what can be recycled:

Mr. Turtle spoke up again, "But, who does all of this? How is it done?"

Andy explained, "There are places called resource recovery facilities or recycling centers where everything is sorted, cleaned, and prepared so it can be used again. Of course, these facilities would not have anything to recycle if people didn't take the time to place the items in the designated places where they should go. Once the recycling items are picked up a process begins to make them reusable. Recycling is important for it can save energy, water and other natural resources where we live.

Did you know that you recycle things too? You take the fallen branches, twigs, and leaves to make your homes or nests. When you do this you make the deep woods look clean and tidy. I bet you never thought about that did you? However, you have nothing to do with what people recycle because you have nothing to do with littering! I am here just to teach you something about all of this because it is my job."

Mrs. Owl spoke up, "We want to thank you Andy. I believe we have learned a great deal about littering and I'm sure we won't forget it. You have made us wiser!"

Sammy saw the serious looks on the faces of his friends and decided to cheer them up. "I have something very important for you to hear! I want you to remember this! CRITTERS DON'T LITTER – PEOPLE DO! Let's say it together loud and clear!"

At that, all the animals began to scamper to their homes and Sammy and Andy smiled as they could hear throughout the deep woods, "CRITTERS DON'T LITTER – PEOPLE DO!"

Andy had done his job well. He taught the animals about littering and recycling. Now he and Sammy could renew their friendship and enjoy their time together.

The End

69651206R20020

Made in the USA
Lexington, KY
04 November 2017